The Baroness and The Pig

THE BARONESS

AND

THE PIG

Michael Mackenzie

Based on characters created by Catherine Fitch and Marion Day

Rock's Mills Press
Oakville, Ontario
2018

Published by
Rock's Mills Press
Oakville, Ontario

Copyright © 1997, 2008, 2018 Michael Mackenzie
Published by arrangement with the author and his agents, Agence M, 388, rue Saint-Jacques, bureau 500-A, Montréal, Québec H2Y 1S1. All rights reserved.

For performance inquiries, please contact Agence M.

Information on this title is available from Rock's Mills Press. Contact us at customer.service@rocksmillspress.com.

www.rocksmillspress.com

Contents

Acknowledgements *by Michael Mackenzie* / vii
Foreword *by Tim Carroll* / ix
"The Enlightened Baroness" *by Leonard Conolly* / xi
Shaw Festival Production, 2018 / xv

THE BARONESS AND THE PIG
Characters / 1
Setting / 2
Photographs / 2
L'Enfant sauvage / 3

ACT ONE / 5
ACT TWO / 47
Staging / 75

Acknowledgements

MICHAEL MACKENZIE

Credit for original development and workshop production goes to The Atelier, The National Arts Centre, Ottawa (1993), with gratitude and very special thanks to Catherine Fitch as the Baroness, Marion Day (development) and Benoit Brière (performance) as Emily, and Gil Osborne, the Atelier director. Also grateful thanks to Tim Carroll and Tim Jennings for bringing the *Baroness* to the Shaw Festival.

Foreword

TIM CARROLL

I first saw *The Baroness and the Pig* in Budapest, almost fifteen years ago. It was called *Elohívás*, which means "Development." The production made great use of the pun in that title, because in Hungarian, as in English, the word can refer to personal growth or a photographic process. A series of photographs were taken and hung up with clips as though drying in a dark room, while the Baroness tried to make the real person lurking unseen within the Pig come into view. It was a beautiful, funny, and sad production, and I was filled with a desire to read the piece in English. My Hungarian was good enough to impress my colleagues in Budapest, where I was directing a play, but not good enough to enjoy all the nuances of the script.

When I returned to England I got hold of the play and found it to be every bit as rich and interesting as I had found it in Hungarian. I subsequently met Michael Mackenzie, through another Hungarian acquaintance (though for reasons totally unrelated to the Budapest production I had seen—all the stage is a world, and a small one), and we hit it off to the extent that he was one of the first people I looked up when I arrived in Canada. I knew that he lived in Montreal, and that couldn't be all that from Toronto, right? They look right next to each other on the map...

One of my aims in taking on the job of leading the Shaw Festival was to redefine our mission with regard to contemporary writing. I have always believed that, considering how many theatres are dedicated to producing new works, it is a shame that there is no theatre dedicated to second productions. It seems to me that, however hard it is to get a first production, it is even harder to get a second. Of course, this is usually because the new play is not good enough (which is not surprising: J.M. Barrie said that writing a play is the hardest thing you can do with a pen in your hand); but at least some of those plays that sink without trace must do so for no good reason. Perhaps they had a bad first production; perhaps they missed the zeitgeist, or were ahead of their time. Whatever the reason, I feel that the Shaw could perform a useful service by unearthing plays that have either had no second production or, like *The Baroness and the Pig*, have been recognised elsewhere but not in Ontario. I am sure that *The Baroness and the Pig* will be seen to be a modern Canadian classic, and I am very proud that we are bringing it to a new audience.

TIM CARROLL IS ARTISTIC DIRECTOR AT THE SHAW FESTIVAL

The Enlightened Baroness

LEONARD CONOLLY

Since Bernard Shaw is, and ever was, the guiding spirit of the Shaw Festival, it is not unreasonable to seek and to reflect on the Shavian spirit in a play that is not likely to be known to Festival audiences. The very title of Michael Mackenzie's *The Baroness and the Pig* has a Shavian ring about it. Shaw liked intriguing titles, titles that prompt audiences to ask "What on earth can *that* be about?" He doesn't have a Baroness in his playlist, but a Duchess appears in *Annajanska, the Wild Grand Duchess*, outranked by the Inca in *The Inca of Perusalem*. And what are we to make of a play with the title of *Passion, Poison, and Petrifaction, or The Fatal Gazogene*? Or *The Simpleton of the Unexpected Isles*? (All of which, incidentally, have been performed at the Shaw Festival.) But while the titles in themselves don't reveal the connection (apart from the whimsical coincidence of the "pyg"), the Shaw play most closely allied thematically to *The Baroness and the Pig* is *Pygmalion*.

Both plays have to do with a person of privilege and authority teaching language and social skills to a seriously disadvantaged person (one having been reared in a French pigsty, the other living in penury in a London slum) to open up opportunities for that person for self-improvement and a degree of economic security. There is, to be sure, a wide divergence between the expected outcomes of the teaching, Eliza's ultimate social aspirations in *Pygmalion* (a lady) far exceeding those of Emily in *The Baroness* (a lady's maid). But the knowledge and skills they acquire are similar: vocabulary, pronunciation, dress codes, social protocols, even a familiarity with Shakespeare (Eliza is taken to a Shakespeare exhibition in London, Emily reads *Julius Caesar* with the Baroness). By the end of each play—and both plays have striking and revelatory endings—we are positioned to judge the results of the educational process for Eliza and Emily. At the same time, inevitably, we assess the teacher as well as the pupil. The contrasting motivations of the two teachers, which are made explicit by each playwright, are instructive. In *Pygmalion*, Henry Higgins, Eliza's teacher, undertakes the education of Eliza to win a bet; in *The Baroness and the Pig*, the Baroness, as she explains in her opening monologue, undertakes the education of Emily as part of what she sees as her "responsibilities to the lower classes." That is, while the social standing of both Higgins and the Baroness isolates them from the rampant inequalities and injustices of their respective societies (London and Paris at the turn of the nineteenth century), it is only the Baroness who takes an enlightened attitude towards those circumstances, albeit with a narrowly defined perspective.

Not only is the Baroness enlightened, she is a child of the Enlightenment, that eighteenth-century "age of reason," during which philosophers such as Jean-Jacques Rousseau insisted on the primacy of rational thought as the basis for liberty and equality. The Baroness particularly remembers her childhood "forbidden reading" of Rousseau's *Émile, ou De l'éducation*, published in 1762 and immediately banned in Paris for its alleged attack on formal religion. In his treatise-cum-novel, Rousseau explored and defined how through education the natural goodness that he and other philosophers believed were possessed by all humans at birth can be protected against the corrupting influences of society. "Tout est bien sortant des mains de l'Auteur des choses, tout dégénère entre les mains de l'homme" is the famous opening sentence of *Émile* ("Everything is good as it leaves the hands of the author of things, everything degenerates in the hands of man"). A carefully constructed educational process (one not dissimilar to that shaped by the Baroness for Emily), will, Rousseau argued, blend nature and reason to create the ideal citizen.

Inspired by Rousseau, and in need of a new maid, the Baroness sets herself the task of transforming "a pure, unsullied creature" into a presentable maid. But where to find such a creature? Higgins encounters

Eliza in the gutters of Covent Garden. Rousseau needed only his imagination to create Émile. But the Baroness recalls a precedent: the case of an *enfant sauvage* being captured (in 1798) in the woods near Aveyron, a village 700 km south of Paris. The child, a boy aged about 11 or 12 who came to be known as Victor, "the wild boy of Aveyron," seems to have been abandoned by his parents. After being caged and publicly exhibited in Paris, Victor was treated by several physicians. The Baroness identifies one such physician, Jean-Marc-Gaspard Itard, who is usually credited with helping Victor reintegrate into society. Itard's *Mémoire et rapport sur Victor de l'Aveyron*, first published in 1801, described his work with Victor. (François Truffaut's 1970 film about Victor, *L'Enfant sauvage*, is based on Itard's book.)

Encouraged by Victor's case ("somewhere in the forests of France was my prodigy!"), the Baroness eventually finds her own *enfant sauvage*, not in a forest but on a farm, an illegitimate girl in a large peasant family who has been put out to live with farm animals, including pigs, "with nothing but a large pair of boots." The Baroness names her Emily, "after Rousseau's *Émile*," she says.

While Emily is named after Émile, her experiences under the tutelage of the Baroness are very different from her counterpart, who lives from birth in a sheltered and safe environment. So does Eliza after coming under Higgins's care, and Victor after coming under Itard's care. The obstacles encountered by Eliza, Émile, and Victor are considerable, but also for the most part predictable, manageable, and surmountable. Not so with Emily. Learning how to set a table is one thing; Emily's unforeseen traumas are quite another and raise questions that neither Rousseau nor Shaw in their fictional narratives contemplated. In Emily's circumstances how is Rousseau's neat balance between nature and reason sustained? What moral imperatives differentiate instinctive behaviour from rational behaviour? How does a pigsty differ from the servants' bedrooms in a French baronial home? What chance have the Baroness's enlightened plans for Emily in the messy human world that is their reality?

Robert Burns, another child of the Enlightenment (of the Scottish variety), provided a cautionary antidote to the age of reason. "The best laid schemes o' mice an' men / Gang aft a-gley," he famously wrote. But what goes awry with the efforts of the Baroness and her maid reflects, perhaps, not so much a negation of enlightenment so much as a determination to resist those forces that would extinguish it. A lesson for our times if ever there was one.

LEONARD CONOLLY IS RESIDENT SCHOLAR AT THE SHAW FESTIVAL

Shaw Festival Production, 2018

This edition of *The Baroness and the Pig* is published in cooperation with the Shaw Festival, Niagara-on-the-Lake, Ontario, where the play was produced from 10 June to 6 October 2018 with the following creative team:

Directed by Selma Dimitrijevic
Designed by Camellia Koo
Lighting designed by Kevin Lamotte
Original music and sound designed by John Gzowski

Yanna McIntosh as the Baroness
Julia Course as Emily

Stage Manager Dora Tomassi
Assistant Stage Manager Bradley Dunn
Production Stage Manager Alison Peddie

Assistant Director Tawiah Ben M'Carthy
Assistant Lighting Designer Chris Malkowski
Voice and Dialect Coach Sarah Shippobotham
Singing Coach Carol Baggott-Forte
Movement Coach Alexis Milligan

The Baroness and The Pig

The Baroness
and
The Pig

© Michael Mackenzie 2008

Characters

THE BARONESS

A lower echelon French aristocrat of a certain age (45?). She is childless and lives with her husband, the Baron, of whom she sees very little. Her principal social contacts are with her servants, but she is often scheming on how to raise her status in her rather sclerotic social milieu.

EMILY

A girl/woman of undetermined age but probably in her mid teens. Born illegitimately to a peasant woman, she was dropped into a pigsty at a very early age and left to fend for herself (not an unheard of event at that time). Her main, if not only, social contacts have been pigs.

Setting

The story takes place in Paris, France, sometime around 1880 to 1890.

The Insertion of "beat" into dialogue implies a short pause or hesitation on behalf of the speaker.

Photographs

From baby pictures to wedding albums, the photograph has been—from the 1850s all the way to the phone selfie—the social record of choice. The camera/phone has scored its inevitable frame around human affairs becoming the ubiquitous legitimation of events and relationships—who stands with whom in the photograph, how they stand, whether they smile; who can be displayed on whose desk at the office, who is cached in whose wallet or phone, who is on the front page of the newspaper, or in the tabloids.

We tend to take the photograph for granted, forgetting that it is not so much a reflection of our world as part of the glue which holds it together. It defines the informal (from holiday snaps to selfies) and the formal (the chairman's portrait). Even the demi-monde of pornography has been inconceivable without the photograph.

Anthropologists found that social groups who were completely unacquainted with photography (and the society it depicted) were unable to decipher these unfamiliar images; photos seemed to them unreadable or—at most—spooky. To be able to "read" them takes a little while. Mind you, the ability to read anything in an arcane society such as the Baroness's could take a little while. We will see... Enter our heroine—Emily.

L'Enfant sauvage

The term *enfant sauvage* comes from a study undertaken by a young French physician, Jean-Marc-Gaspard Itard, at the end of the eighteenth century. It refers to children raised outside of human contact and society, often by animals.

The debate still rages as to how we might understand the humanity of such individuals. Although they often have the social and personal characteristics of the animals that raised them and a limited comprehension of symbolic activities (such as language), they have a powerful intelligence for imitation and sometimes a strong emotional attachment to the milieu they were raised in.

Act One

Scene One

First Photograph

The BARONESS addresses the audience.

EMILY is slumped on the floor quite still with a pair of filthy boots on her feet. As she's under a filthy blanket we can see very little of her—she is more a shape than anything else. Maybe some soft grunting noises.

The Baroness checks/prepares herself throughout the following for a photograph. She does not acknowledge the presence of/sounds of Emily until the very end of the scene.

BARONESS

> After the unfortunate departure of our third downstairs maid this year, I began the wearisome task of casting about for a suitable replacement. Quite aside from this, I had been . . . pondering our responsibilities to the lower classes. My friends . . . my husband . . . dismissed these reflections. And then it struck me. I could set an example in the choice of a maid. What, I thought, if I could show my friends that the meanest of human beings could be brought on to understand the virtues of service. There would be sacrifices in such an undertaking. Downstairs maids must be neat, mannerly and presentable, even pretty. I would educate her in all the appropriate social graces. Pretty is simply the dictate of fashion. Pretty can be a disadvantage. All our other maids were pretty.

Beat.

How inspiring such a project could be to others. I remembered my forbidden reading as a young girl of Jean-Jacques Rousseau's *Émile*. The bringing out of a pure, unsullied creature into the world. Where could I find such a one? Then I came across Dr Itard's account of the *enfant sauvage*, the child raised by wild beasts and then brought back to society.

What an inspiration! This would be my project. There, somewhere in the forests of France was my prodigy!

Beat.

Unfortunately, no one seemed to be in contact with any suitable children. Finally she was found. Raised by domestic animals, the illegitimate daughter from a large peasant family who had put her out, with nothing but a large pair of boots. Not from the forests but from the farmyard. And I will call her Emily, after Rousseau's *Émile*. Emily!

The Baroness taps the blanket, Emily's face appears. She makes grunting sounds.

CAMERA FLASH. *She squeals. Blackout.*

Scene Two

First Interview—The Table

Emily is crouched on the floor in a maid's outfit and her boots, rubbing against the furniture. She is mouthing a phrase, "Madam la Baroness." Enter the Baroness. She sees Emily—a certain degree of surprise; she wasn't expecting to run into this. Perhaps she is deciding to leave when . . .

EMILY

    Madam la Baroness!

Emily speaks as if the words (something new for her) are objects in her mouth.

BARONESS

Stops.

    Yes, I am the Baroness. Now you mustn't . . . grovel like that.

EMILY

    Grovel . . . Boots.

BARONESS

    Yes, boots. Now up you get.

Motions several times at Emily who finally gets it and stands up very awkwardly.

EMILY

    Standing!

BARONESS

Yes standing, very good.

Pause.

Perhaps a little more so.

Baroness motions to correct posture. Emily stares at the Baroness's hands and wobbles into a more upright position.

Excellent, excellent! Progress.

EMILY

Madam la Baroness!

BARONESS

Yes?...Yes. Jeannette has done quite well...a beginning.

Looking at boots.

Unfortunate... But they are clean at least.

EMILY

Soap.

BARONESS

For the first time it seems.

Pause. Attempt at casual conversation.

Jeannette tells me you like to sleep *under* the bed.

No reaction from Emily.

Did she tell you your name?

No reaction.

> . . . Your name?

EMILY

Quietly.

> Madam la—

BARONESS

Interrupting.

> Emily. Your name is Emily.

Indicates Emily.

> Em-il-y.

EMILY

Exactly the same intonation.

> Em-il-y.

BARONESS

> Emily.

Emily gets closer to study the Baroness's mouth. The Baroness adopts evasive movements.

EMILY

> Emily.

BARONESS

> Yes, very good. Now stand up straight Emily. You must stand up straight. Jeannette has done very well in the past month teaching you to . . . stand, and so forth.

Beat.

> Now, I have given some serious thought to your education and we shall start with the . . .

Indicating table.

> . . . table.

Emily makes a pig noise.

BARONESS (CONT'D)

> Don't make that noise please Emily.

The mentor.

> Now. The table, Emily, is where we meet and enjoy our friends.

EMILY

Looks at it.

> Table.

BARONESS

> The table.

EMILY

> The table.

BARONESS

> For dinner.

EMILY

Getting excited.

> Dinner . . . ?

BARONESS

> Not now.

Emily makes her noise.

BARONESS (CONT'D)

> Emily, we must act properly.

EMILY

> Act properly . . .

To mentor.

> Acting properly is very important. It is, perhaps, the nub.

During the following Emily begins to massage her groin. The Baroness, carried away, doesn't notice.

BARONESS (CONT'D)

> You must act properly . . . only move when you are asked to move. You must only speak to announce guests. And before you leave you will always say, "Will that be all, Madam?"

Turns to see Emily is rubbing her groin.

BARONESS (CONT'D)

>Don't do that!!

Emily freezes.

>Jeannette will be instructing you on laying the table.

EMILY

>Laying the table.

Emily leans over to sniff, perhaps gnaw or lay on the table.

BARONESS

>Emily!

To herself.

>No, no. We knew this would be trying.

To Emily.

>Leave the table!

Emily leaves the table alone.

BARONESS (CONT'D)

>Lay the table means to set the table to prepare it. So we can eat dinner at the table.

EMILY

Encouraged.

>Dinner.

BARONESS

So dinner might be served.

EMILY

Dinner?

BARONESS

Jeannette can show you the correct table settings, for the cutlery.

EMILY

Dinner?

BARONESS

And then will be feeding you.

Emily grunts.

BARONESS (CONT'D)

Don't make that noise.

Sighs.

Difficult times. But one day, one day when we have a particularly auspicious gathering—perhaps again the Prince of Wales . . .

Emily starts rubbing herself on the furniture.

BARONESS (CONT'D)

. . . I shall say, "I must now introduce Emily." "Duchess de Sagan?" She will still be talking. A hush, " . . . the maid?!" And then I will tell your story, our story. The savage beast, tamed. And they will wonder, they will be amazed.

Baroness turns to see Emily rubbing away. Beat.

BARONESS (CONT'D)

We have much to do Emily.

Emily looks up, stops rubbing.

But so far I am quite pleased.

Sits.

You may go now, Emily.

Beat.

The interview is over.

Beat.

What should you say? You should say "Will that be all, Madam?" . . . "Will that be all, Madam?"

EMILY

Exact intonation.

"Will that be all, Madam?"

Stands motionless.

BARONESS

Yes. Thank you.

Intonation.

"Yes. Thank you."

Pause.

BARONESS

Good. You may tell Jeannette I will be in the library.

The Baroness exits. Emily looks around her.

Scene Three

Maid Encounters Cutlery

Emily is alone standing at the table with cutlery. She seems very ineffectually trying to clean it with a cloth. A piece drops on the floor. As she picks it up she catches sight of herself in the mirror. She reacts as if Jeannette had just walked in to the room. She goes back to her inept cleaning.

Scene Four

Second Interview—The Settings

Emily is standing as if threatened not to move. The table has one setting. Baroness is surveying Emily.

BARONESS

Well, yes. Good. Jeannette tells me, that while we have been wintering in Italy, someone has been doing quite well, downstairs.

Baroness takes a long look at the boots.

BARONESS (CONT'D)

I hear that we still don't want to wear the footwear that has been specially bought for us?

EMILY

We... don't...?

BARONESS

We don't want to take our boots off.

EMILY

Madam boots.

BARONESS

Emily's boots. I don't wear boots. See, I am wearing this very nice comfortable footwear, as Emily could be doing...?

Beat.

Well, Jeannette has done quite well.

EMILY

Dinner.

BARONESS

Dinner?

EMILY

Jeannette...

BARONESS

What?

She gets it.

Ah yes, Jeannette gives you dinner. Emily, you must learn to speak in complete sentences. For example, "Jeannette . . . gives . . . me . . . dinner."

BARONESS (CONT'D)

Soon you will be learning to announce my guests and that must be done clearly, with dignity. So you should speak in sentences, as in . . . "Jeannette gives me dinner" . . .

EMILY

You dinner?

BARONESS

No. She gives you dinner.

Beat.

Say, "Jeannette gives me dinner."

EMILY

Jeannette, gives, you . . . big dinner?

BARONESS

Jeannette doesn't give me dinner, she gives *you* dinner.

EMILY

Sympathetic.

    No dinner for you?

BARONESS

    Yes, Emily I have dinner! Now. Jeannette tells me that you have been learning the settings for the table.

EMILY

    Cutlery.

BARONESS

    So Emily. How many forks are there?

EMILY

    Three forks.

BARONESS

    And what are they?

Pause.

BARONESS (CONT'D)

    The first one?

EMILY

Beat.

    Salad fork!

BARONESS

> Good. Excellent! And the next one . . . ? The big one, in the middle . . . The next fork. It's a . . .

EMILY

Beat.

> Dinner fork!

BARONESS

> Excellent! And the last one? It's a . . . The littlest one, on the inside, it's a . . . it's a . . .

Mouths "desert fork."

EMILY

Beat.

> Desert fork.

BARONESS

> I think this is going to work out splendidly, splendidly.

EMILY

> Count the cutlery.

BARONESS

> Yes! You count the cutlery . . . a very important task.

EMILY

> Fifty-five salad forks, fifty-five dinner forks, fifty-five desert forks.

BARONESS

> Excellent. Most gratifying, Emily. Soon I hope you will understand what a trust and responsibility this is. Inventory is the cornerstone of any properly run household, one might say of modern civilization itself. My husband, the Baron, spends much of his time taking inventories of the resources of African countries that the natives overlooked.

Emily has noticed a button on the floor. Goes over and picks it up.

BARONESS (CONT'D)

> You don't have to do that. The cleaning maid can do that.

Emily puts it in her mouth.

BARONESS (CONT'D)

> Emily!

Emily spits it out on to the floor. Baroness shudders.

Pause.

BARONESS (CONT'D)

> So you in your small way are becoming part of society. Perhaps I shall ask Jeannette to trust you with folding the sheets.

Baroness exits.

EMILY

Will that be all, Madam?

Scene Five

Folding the Sheets

Emily, alone, confronted with a pile of unfolded sheets. She very awkwardly starts to try to fold them. She begins to smell them. As she continues, she begins to get seduced by the smell of the sheets. She begins to masturbate.

Scene Six

Taking Away Emily's Boots

Emily is on the floor, breathless, clutching her boots, and wearing stockings for the first time. We have the impression a struggle might have just taken place. Enter Baroness holding new boots . . . er, footwear.

BARONESS

Mock cross.

> Jeannette is very upset. She says you tried to bite her. Just because of some silly boots. She's going to get the chauffeur.

Emily is unmoved.

BARONESS (CONT'D)

Change of strategy.

> I don't think she showed you your new nice footwear we've had specially made for you. We're going to have our photograph taken tomorrow, Emily. Together. You want to look your best, don't you?

Baroness realizes that Emily is staring at the new boots. She carefully puts them down in front of Emily.

BARONESS (CONT'D)

    You see. Why don't you put them on?

Pause. Emily reaches for the boots, letting her own drop. She examines them. Encouraged by the Baroness, she pulls them halfway on her feet. She's quite pleased; wiggles her feet with the new boot perched on them.

BARONESS (CONT'D)

    There! A lot of fuss about nothing. Now we just have to get rid of the nasty old ones.

Baroness goes to leave, changes her mind, takes out a handkerchief and uses it to pick up Emily's old boots. As soon as she lifts them—a complete animal snarl from Emily. She dives at the Baroness who drops the boots and screams.

BARONESS (CONT'D)

    Jeannette!!

Snap lights to black.

Scene Seven

Taking a Photograph

Baroness, a little tense. She is preparing, as in Scene 1, for a photograph. She adjusts her clothing, etc. She is waiting for Emily. Emily enters in the new (heeled) shoes—a pig on stilts. With great difficulty she negotiates her way to stand by the Baroness as best she can. They pose.

FLASH.

Emily reacts, eyes squeezed shut, hands reaching, flashes continue as the pose falls apart in a series of increasingly chaotic freezes.

Scene Eight

Learning to Answer the Door

The Baroness is sitting. She is drinking some wine. Enter Emily.

BARONESS

Ah, Emily. Today we begin a very important part of your education—we will learn to announce my guests. Now, in my position, as you have probably understood, there are many who wish to call, to pay their respects. And I receive them, those who are entitled to the honour. Of course we have the pretenders, the Nouveau Riche who call in an attempt to better their position, such as M. Voisine. To him you simply say, "No."

EMILY

"No" to M. Voisine. Pretender.

BARONESS

Exactly. A charlatan. Now, there will be a ring at the door—our new, electrical bell. You will answer the door.

EMILY

The door rings. Answer . . . ?

BARONESS

Yes.

EMILY

Ri-ing!

Bell sound.

BARONESS

You don't ring.

EMILY

Door rings. Answer, "ring" . . . ?

BARONESS

You simply go to the door and open it. That is answering the door.

Gets up, mimes action.

You go to the door you open it and you curtsy, as Jeannette has shown you.

Emily curtsies.

BARONESS (CONT'D)

> . . . And there will be someone there. If they are familiar . . . and we will learn their names . . . you may allow them to enter the foyer. "Please enter."

Demonstrative movement.

EMILY

> "Please enter."

Exactly the same intonation and movement.

BARONESS

> Exactly. Then you will say, "Who may I say is calling . . . ?"

EMILY

> "Who may I say is calling . . . ?"

BARONESS

> . . . And they will tell you, and may hand you a card, and . . . oh yes, you will have a tray, this tray in fact.

She picks up a small, highly polished silver tray and gives it to Emily.

BARONESS (CONT'D)

> This is the card tray.

EMILY

Looks in the tray, immediately taken.

> Emily's tray.

BARONESS

> Alright, it's Emily's tray. They will place the card on the tray.

EMILY

She really likes the tray.

> Emily's tray . . . ?

BARONESS

> Then you will say, "Wait here. I will see if the Baroness is at home."

EMILY

Still preoccupied by the tray.

> "I will see if the Baroness is at home."

Pause. Emily is falling in love with the tray.

BARONESS

> Emily . . . ?

EMILY

> Emily's tray.

BARONESS

> Hold it out, for the card.

Emily holds it at arm's length.

BARONESS (CONT'D)

> Hold it like this.

She goes to take the tray but finds Emily has it in her vice-like grip. A small struggle ensues. The Baroness finally wrestles the tray from the Emily by twisting it. She straightens her clothes and then demonstrates.

BARONESS (CONT'D)

Holding out the tray.

"Who may I say is calling?"

EMILY

Emily is calling.

Grabs hold of the tray.

With her tray. Baroness is home?

BARONESS

Off guard.

What?

EMILY

My card.

Leans over and licks the tray.

BARONESS

Don't lick the tray!

Beat. Taking that to mean she should lick something else, Emily goes to lick Baroness.

BARONESS (CONT'D)

　No!

Pause. Baroness recovers, surrenders the tray to Emily

　Now take the tray.

Emily takes it.

　Good. Hold it properly.

Perhaps the Baroness needs a quick drink.

BARONESS (CONT'D)

　Let's start again . . .

Beat.

　The guest arrives. Emily answers the door.

EMILY

　Ri-ing!

BARONESS

　I told you not to ring!

EMILY

　Not Emily ring, the door rings.

Emily answers it.

　"Open the door" . . .

BARONESS

　Alright, yes.

EMILY

Adopts exact position and intonation.

"Who may I say is calling?"

BARONESS

Yes. Now imagine I am the caller—You may say . . . "the Duchess de Sagan is calling. Here is my card."

EMILY

Thank you. Don't lick the tray.

BARONESS

We don't say that.

EMILY

Offering tray.

Lick . . . ?

BARONESS

No! We don't lick trays.

EMILY

Thinks. Offers her arm.

Emily . . . ?

BARONESS

No!!

Emily takes back her arm. Licks it. Not crazy about the taste.

EMILY

Agreeing with Baroness.

    No. Soapy.

BARONESS

Control. Breathes. Drink?

    Let's start again.

EMILY

Enjoying herself.

    Yes!

BARONESS

    Now. There is a ring at the door.

EMILY

    Ri-ing!

BARONESS

Breathes.

    And you pick up the tray . . .

EMILY

    Emily's tray.

BARONESS

    . . . and go to the door. You open the door, and what do you say?

EMILY

Adopting position and intonation.

"Who may I say is calling?"

BARONESS

Good. And the guest gives you their name and places the card on the tray, so. To which you answer . . . ?

EMILY

Don't answer, just open the door.

BARONESS

You do answer!

EMILY

Ri-ing!

BARONESS

Losing it.

Think Emily! Use your head! "Please wait here. I will see if the Baroness is at home!"

EMILY

Exactly the tone of the Baroness losing it.

"Please wait here. I will see if the Baroness is at home!"

Silence. The Baroness moves on.

BARONESS

Then you enter my room, present the card . . .

Emily turns around and presents the tray.

BARONESS (CONT'D)

Good. And I will tell you if I am home or not.

EMILY

Has to think about this one.

Baroness not at home . . . ?

BARONESS

Perhaps.

EMILY

Gone out?

BARONESS

No. I'm simply not at home to whoever . . . may be calling.

EMILY

She turns around.

Baroness says she is not home.

BARONESS

You just say . . . I am not home.

EMILY

"Emily's not home. Baroness is not home." Baroness out with Emily?

BARONESS

>No! We are both home. We simply . . . *pretend* I am not home.

EMILY

>Charlatan?

Silence.

BARONESS

>Let's start again.

EMILY

>Yes! Ri-ing!

Quietly to herself.

>Not Emily ring, door ring.

Back to performance.

>Answer the door. "No" to M. Voisine. "Please wait. I will see if Baroness is home." Wait for card on Emily's tray. Use my head.

Pauses to think about this one, then bangs the tray on her head.

>Go to Baroness room.

Presents tray to Baroness.

>Here's card.

Quietly to herself.

>Emily's tray.

Back to performance.

Is Madam pretending she's home?

Scene Nine

Emily in the Mirror

Emily carrying sheets passes in front of the mirror, curtsies, goes on. She stops, aware this is not quite as it seems to her. Then goes back to check it out. She approaches the mirror carefully, sniffs, tries to look behind the mirror, licks the mirror, doesn't like it, keeps going.

Scene Ten

The Theatre

Emily is cleaning cutlery—including some large, sharp knives at the table. Enter the Baroness. She is elated and perhaps a little drunk, and clearly still enraptured by a performance she has just attended. She carries a small copy of Shakespeare's Julius Caesar *and wears her evening cloak.*

BARONESS

Ah, Emily. Dear Emily. We have been to the theatre, the theatre.

EMILY

> The theatre.

BARONESS

> Shakespeare. Such delicacy, such gravity. "What a thing is man," Emily. "What a thing is man."

EMILY

> Baron . . . ?

BARONESS

> No, no. I speak of "man" . . . in general . . . Man.

Emily doesn't get it, but the Baroness's enthusiasm is infectious.

BARONESS (CONT'D)

> The theatre. We see Man, we see the world, we see ourselves, and we are purged.

EMILY

> See ourself.

BARONESS

> The Mirror of Tragedy.

Removing her cloak and dumping it in Emily's arms.

> This evening we saw *The Tragedy of Julius Caesar*. And in that one great man and his story we see ourselves. That spare stage for one brief moment in time carries the weight of us all. Humanity.

Emily, quite excited, makes her noise.

BARONESS (CONT'D)

Don't make that noise, Emily. I've told you.

EMILY

Very sorry, Madam.

Pause. Wanting to get things going again.

On a stage?

BARONESS

Emily, dear. The theatre—the stage—is a place where people act.

EMILY

"Act properly."

BARONESS

They don't act properly! I mean they do act properly.

Pause as she thinks how to explain.

There are people, actors who take on . . . roles. They pretend they are other people—historical figures for example, like Julius Caesar. And they act out the . . . story.

EMILY

Julius Caesar. He will be calling. Is madam home?

BARONESS

Of course he won't be calling, he's dead!

EMILY

    M. Voisine pretends. I say, "Madam isn't home."

BARONESS

    I give up, I do really.

Sigh of the put upon.

    Oh Emily. You are my trial and I must persevere.

Preparing for her pedagogical task, the Baroness thinks and then prepares to set the stage.

BARONESS (CONT'D)

    We go to the theatre, we greet our friends . . .

Mime.

    And we seat ourselves . . .

She sits on the sofa indicates Emily to join her. Emily, fascinated, tentatively does so.

BARONESS (CONT'D)

    You see here we are at the theatre, amongst our friends and acquaintances . . .

Mime greetings.

    . . . waiting for the actors. There is the stage and the actors are preparing.

EMILY

    Dinner?

BARONESS

> No, not dinner. They are putting on costumes and make-up, for the performance.

She sees Emily has no idea what she's talking about.

BARONESS (CONT'D)

> Imagine we are the actors and we are preparing. Imagine, sheer fancy of course, that the playwright has written a play about me, focusing on some heroic or worthy action I may have performed.

The Baroness pulls Emily to her feet and puts the cloak on her.

BARONESS (CONT'D)

> You are the actor. Now, here is your costume. You see! And now you are the Baroness, you must act the part, you must become me.

The Baroness sits expectantly to watch.

EMILY

> Me, the Baroness?

BARONESS

> Yes, that's it.

A long focused pause as Emily with great intensity becomes the Baroness as completely as possible—voice, intonation, posture.

EMILY

"I give up, I do really."

Sigh.

"Oh Emily. You are my trial and I must persevere."

She does the Baroness's sad look at Emily. Shocked silence.

BARONESS

Unnerved.

Well, yes . . . yes that's it. Indeed.

EMILY

You're the maid?

BARONESS

No I'm not going to be the maid. You can take it off now. The cloak, you can take it off.

Emily becomes Emily again, taking off the cloak.

BARONESS (CONT'D)

Good. Well, yes.

Off balance, but trying to get back into the mood the Baroness sits, picks up the copy of the play.

BARONESS (CONT'D)

This evening the Baron and myself saw an excellent play portraying the fatal envy of the common lot for their betters. Shakespeare shows it all. Humanity, its most noble and most base instincts.

EMILY

Very keen to get back in the mood.

   Julius Caesar.

BARONESS

   A great man, a man of vision, a man beloved ... killed by the conspirators.

EMILY

Finds a word.

   How?

BARONESS

   Stabbed by envious knives, even by those who profess to love him best. Julius Caesar comes to the Senate, ignoring all portends and omens, fearing nothing.

Begins to take on the role.

   His arrival is hailed by a grateful people. He enters the Senate and there ...

BARONESS (CONT'D)

Indicates Emily.

   ... are the conspirators hiding their black hearts behind fine words of welcome.

EMILY

Indicating herself.

   Conspirator?

BARONESS

Yes, Emily. Imagine yourself a conspirator. You and your cohorts are plotting my death, you will surround me, wooing me to a false sense of security with base sycophantic groveling...

EMILY

As she grovels.

Groveling...

BARONESS

Not quite so much groveling... Yes. And then when my back is turned you kill me.

EMILY

Knife.

BARONESS

Exactly, the knife!

Emily makes her noise, reproving gesture from Julius Caesar a.k.a. the Baroness.

BARONESS (CONT'D)

I am Caesar entering the Senate, and as I enter you come up to me.

She reads from the play.

"... Most high and mighty Caesar..."

Prompting Emily.

"Most high and mighty Caesar . . ."

EMILY

"Most high and mighty Caesar!"

BARONESS

Good, good! "These couchings and these lowly courtesies / Might fire the blood of ordinary men." You see, such power, such command.

Emily is thrilled by all this attention and action.

BARONESS (CONT'D)

"Caesar doth not wrong, nor without cause will be satisfied." Now, you kiss my hand. "I kiss thy hand, but not in flattery great Caesar."

EMILY

"I kiss thy hand, but not in flattery great Caesar!"

BARONESS

"I could well be moved if I were as you / If I could pray to move prayers would move me." "The skies are painted with unnumbered sparks. / They all of fire and every one doth shine, / But there's one in all that doth hold its place."

Emily, behind the Baroness's back, picks out of the cutlery a large, very sharp-looking knife.

BARONESS (CONT'D)

"So in this world which is furnished well with men / And men are flesh and blood and apprehensive / Yet in that number I do know but one . . . "

Baroness turns and and almost runs into the knife that Emily, standing right there, is brandishing. Baroness and Emily look at each other. Baroness screams?

Snap to black.

Scene Eleven

First Rape

Dark. The Baroness's voice.

BARONESS

Emily, Emily.

Pause. Lights up slowly on Baroness in a dark corridor.

BARONESS (CONT'D)

Jeannette has asked me to speak to you. This is very irregular, having to enter the servants quarters like this. Emily. Are you ill? Jeannette said you haven't left your room this morning . . . you have not done your jobs. She said you snarled at her when she tried to come in to see you.

Baroness stoops to pick something up, it's the Baron's hat.

BARONESS (CONT'D)

Are you ill? Emily. I'm coming in.

Baroness enters.

It's morning, we should draw back the blinds.

She does so with a gesture.

Lights up. Emily is lying motionless on the bed awake in a corset and shift, gripping a sheet between her legs.

She seems to be in pain.

The Baroness sees something on the floor, she reaches down and picks up a cigar butt with disgust. (Or find another way to stage the Baron's recent presence.)

Emily grunts in pain.

BARONESS (CONT'D)

Rounding on Emily in absolute fury.

> Don't . . . make . . . that . . . sound! I . . . told . . . you . . . not . . . to make that sound!

She furiously rips the sheet away from Emily—it has blood on it.

BARONESS (CONT'D)

Quietly.

> I told you not to do that. I told you . . .

She sits at the end of Emily's bed.

Scene Twelve

Baroness Looks at her Album

Baroness is sitting looking at a rather grand album of photos.

BARONESS

Studying the album.

> This is our photographic album. I conceived it myself. As a young girl I had a sketch album and I thought, "Why not a photographic album, as a true portrait of our family life?" So here we have all our occasions, the marriage and afterwards—in order, each picture perfectly placed. My husband took the early photographs, but now he is preoccupied with art photography, and business. This . . .

Blank page.

> . . . is where Emily's photograph is to go, and I hoped that one day she might see and appreciate her position in the family album.

Looking closely at the album.

> But I'm not quite sure exactly where it fits in.

Change focus to Emily in bed (under the bed?). She is playing with her reflection in the tray.

Then—cataclysmically—she slowly realizes it's her—it's her reflection, it's Emily in the mirror. She is astounded. She takes one huge step towards being human.

Fade to black.

END OF ACT ONE

Act Two

Scene One

A Trip to the Country

Lights up slowly to reveal Baroness and Emily in the country (outskirts of Paris). Emily is carrying a picnic basket, and blanket under one arm and a small folding chair under the other.

The Baroness is carrying a sketch pad. Her attitude towards Emily is one of absolute deference, as if she were deeply apologetic.

Emily hardly moves, ecstatically engrossed in the smells, eyes closed. This is the first time she's been outside since arriving at the Baroness's house.

BARONESS

This will do I suppose. Such a nice view of the . . .

Squints.

. . . railway. And the river. Emily?

No response.

Emily.

Goes to take chair, she can't budge Emily.

Emily? Emily!

Emily drops the chair but has no other reaction as she carries on ecstatically sniffing.

BARONESS (CONT'D)

Takes chair, opens it and sits.

    Well.

Pause.

    I thought it would be nice for you to get into the fresh air.

Squints into the distance. Beat.

    Emily?

Emily drops the basket, but still is transfixed, smelling.

BARONESS (CONT'D)

    It's really quite hard to find somewhere to go, just you and me—on impulse. I thought it would be nice to be together, the two of us.

EMILY

    Smell.

Baroness tentatively sniffs the air.

    Smell. Farm smell.

BARONESS

    Yes, it is, isn't it.

Pause.

BARONESS (CONT'D)

    Would you like to . . .

Shrugs.

... run around? I don't think they worry about that sort of thing out here.

Pause.

Emily, what would you like to do? Would you like to sit down, I brought your blanket.

EMILY

Sit?

BARONESS

If you like.

Pause.

What would you like to do?

Emily looks at her as if to confirm she has carte blanche. Beat. Then drops to her hands and knees sniffing the grass, very quietly grunting.

The Baroness is shocked, she looks around, embarrassed, as much for Emily's deep emotional state as for the gesture itself.

Pause. The Baroness gets out her sketch pad.

BARONESS (CONT'D)

I brought my sketching pad.

EMILY

To herself, absorbed in the grass.

Emily.

BARONESS

Taking this as a request to be sketched.

    Oh, alright.

She moves her chair back and begins to sketch Emily.

BARONESS (CONT'D)

To herself, with pauses, speaking her thoughts as she sketches.

    I've never been very good, that's one of the reasons I gave up. And married women don't do that sort of thing. Then I saw these paintings, you see, not in the Academy, just some odd Bohemian artists . . . very odd. Sort of blotchy and blurry. And I thought, well if they can do it, and charge good money, why shouldn't I make my little sketches?

Emily has dropped her head so she can smell the grass better.

BARONESS (CONT'D)

    You're going to have to be still if I'm going to draw you. Why don't you make yourself comfortable.

Emily flops full out on her front burying her head in the grass, sniffing.

The Baroness hesitates and then self-consciously starts again.

As before.

    I forgot how much I enjoyed this. So it's a good thing I saw those funny paintings. The odd thing was not just how they painted, but the things they painted. Nothing about . . . humanity. Just people. Who weren't even being painted, I mean they were being painted. But it was if it didn't matter, they didn't care. You see in a painting—a proper painting, or a photograph—you can always see who someone is right away.

For the first time in the play the Baroness is not posing at all. Emily quacks. Baroness starts, looks around.

BARONESS (CONT'D)

Seeing off in the distance.

Ah yes, so there are. Did you . . . smell them?

EMILY

Quack.

BARONESS

Yes, there are. Ducks.

EMILY

Quack.

BARONESS

Ducks.

Emily settles down again. Pause.

BARONESS (CONT'D)

Reflectively.

Quack. And that was the other thing about those paintings sometimes they just seemed to crowd everything in—ducks, railways, buildings with chimneys, people walking, bathers . . . Everything thrown in. As if they all belonged together.

She looks at her sketch.

To herself.

 Emily.

Emily kneels up.

EMILY

To herself.

 Me.

BARONESS

Taking this as a comment.

 It actually looks more like a duck.

Shows it to Emily. Fade to black.

Scene Two

Two Photographs

The Baroness opens a letter. She reads with increasing concern and then alarm. She looks in the envelope as if directed to by something she has read. Two photos fall out. She slowly bends and picks them up. She looks at them and then lets them fall—shocked and clearly horrified.

Blackout.

Scene Three

Letter from a Well-Wisher

Emily enters Baroness's room where the Baroness is sitting in half dark. There are the two photographs on the floor. The Baroness is holding a half-crumpled letter. Emily deposits a cloth, draws some blinds, and light pours in. The Baroness squeezes her eyes shut, blinded by the light. Emily curtsies, and goes to leave.

BARONESS

Completely drunk. Suppressed rage.

> I have a letter Emily. Its from a well-wisher . . . a well-wisher. A vile-minded person who dares call themselves a well-wisher to me! To me, the Baroness. They say . . . they say, such things about . . . me. They talk of the Baron . . . with women of the streets, with servants. They have disgusting pictures, they say his pictures . . . And they say "how predictable, how predictable," because I am "dried up," I have no "passion." I! I? No passion! How dare they. They think passion is primitive . . . animal savagery. They think I have no passion. And they laugh, they laugh at me . . .

Focuses on the photographs with utter rage and humiliation. Pause. Holds the letter out to Emily.

> Eat it! Eat the letter! You eat . . . things, animal. Eat the letter.

Emily is silent and, as much as she can be, shocked.

BARONESS (CONT'D)

> Eat it!

EMILY

Emily . . . ?

BARONESS

Animal! Eat it!

EMILY

Emily . . . animal.

BARONESS

Savage! Pig!

EMILY

Emily . . . pig?

BARONESS

I'm a woman! A passionate woman.

EMILY

We act . . . Conspirator?

BARONESS

You. You'd be nothing. I made you everything you are. You'd be back in your pigsty slime with nothing but your filthy boots. You want to go back there? Today! you could be back there today.

EMILY

I announce the guests. "Please wait." "Madam is not home." I count the cutlery—one, two, three—

BARONESS

Falling to her knees. Grabs a photograph.

Eat them!

Holds out photograph. Emily very slowly puts her mouth to it.

BARONESS (CONT'D)

Like this, animal!

Tears the photograph with her own mouth.

Like a savage animal.

Baroness tears the photographs with her mouth and hands. She stops, breaks, breathing heavily, face down in front of Emily. Pause.

EMILY

Will that be all, Madam?

Baroness reaches out and holds EMILY's foot. Pause.

BARONESS

Quietly.

Emily's boots. Emily has no boots.

EMILY

No boots.

BARONESS

Poor Emily.

Scene Four

Emily Tears the Sheets

Emily is with the sheets again. Start as in Act 1, Scene 5, but now she is better at folding.

At the point in Scene 5 where she began to masturbate, she very deliberately starts to tear the sheet. Fade.

Scene Five

The Baroness Can't Sleep

Baroness is sitting on a sofa in her nightgown late at night.

Enter Emily looking sleepy. She appears very cold towards Baroness. Baroness is uncomfortable, embarrassed. There is wine beside her and an open box of candies.

BARONESS

>I sent for you because I thought you might sit with me for a while. I don't seem to be able to sleep.

EMILY

>Emily sleep.

BARONESS

>Yes I know. But I thought you might sit with me a while. I thought you might enjoy that.

EMILY

>Sit?

BARONESS

Yes. You may sit.

Emily warily sits next to the Baroness.

BARONESS (CONT'D)

I really shouldn't be doing this. If I asked any of the other servants to sit with me, I know it would make them presumptuous and give them ideas above their station. But in your case Emily, I know there will be no presumption.

EMILY

Has noticed the Baroness's bon-bons.

Bon-bons . . . ?

BARONESS

Yes, bon-bons. You see I can offer you a bon-bon and you will not see it as an avenue to take advantage.

Emily can't believe her luck. Interrogatively indicates the bon-bons.

BARONESS (CONT'D)

Yes you may.

Emily gets to it. Loud, appreciative noises.

BARONESS (CONT'D)

Yes . . . well. They are good. I have them made up by my confectioner. I am glad you enjoy them.

Beat.

You see, Emily, I know I could even offer you a glass of wine, and this would not be seen as an act of weak indulgence, to be gossiped about below stairs.

Beat.

Would you like some wine, Emily . . . Emily?

She gets Emily a glass of wine. Emily can't believe it, takes it delicately, awkwardly.

BARONESS (CONT'D)

Now we are drinking wine together, the Baroness and the maid. A toast, a toast to our project which will make us—both . . . respected. Like this . . .

Demonstrates toasting to Emily.

Emily sips. Reaction, cough, but she likes it.

BARONESS (CONT'D)

Good.

Pause.

You might read to me, if you could read.

EMILY

Read the cards.

BARONESS

I know. But only after someone's told you what's on them. Perhaps I could read to you.

EMILY

> *Julius Caesar?*

BARONESS

> I don't think so Emily.

Sudden thought.

> From my diary! I have always kept a diary.

BARONESS (CONT'D)

She gets up to look for her diary.

> Here, you see. This is a long time ago. When I was young . . . er, younger.

Opening the diary.

> The Opera! The first time at the opera! The singing, the costumes, dancing. It was so . . . different then. I wasn't the Baroness. I was just a girl, like you. Well, not quite like you.

EMILY

> *Singing.*

BARONESS

> Beautiful singing. Here.

Reading.

> "I was so overcome that I wept and continued to do so all the way home in the carriage, till Mama told me quite sharply that was enough and I would bloodshot my eyes. But I still wept later in my room for Mignon, the lovely

young girl exiled from her country home. This morning my eyes are a little bloodshot. I shall avoid Mama, but I am resolved to steal away and buy the sheet music for Mignon's sad song longing for her homeland." And I did! And I taught it to myself without Mama ever knowing. No one knew in fact, except me. I would sing it for . . . myself . . .

Baroness sings the first line of Connais-tu le pays *from the opera* Mignon *by Ambroise Thomas.*

EMILY

Singing.

BARONESS

Yes. Yes! So much, when I was younger . . . before I was the Baroness. We would . . .

EMILY

Sing.

The Baroness sings the line again for Emily. Beat. Emily repeats the line perfectly.

BARONESS

Yes. Well, that's it.

EMILY

Sing more.

BARONESS

Well . . . then it goes . . .

Baroness sings the next line. Emily repeats. A bit loud. Baroness signals to be a little quieter. Continue till they are through a part of the song.

BARONESS (CONT'D)

> Remarkable Emily. You do have a melodious voice. Untutored but very . . . melodious. You would have loved it, the Opera. The singing, the dances.

EMILY

> Dances.

BARONESS

> Yes.

EMILY

> How?

BARONESS

> Well . . .

Hesitates.

> Well, . . .

Stands.

> . . . like this.

Baroness does a gentle solo. Emily stands, imitates, Baroness takes the glass from her. They dance. Emily stumbles Baroness catches her, they dance together. Baroness hums accompaniment.

After a while they're a bit breathless and they sit. Pause.

EMILY

　Sing more.

BARONESS

　Yes. But quietly, as the rest of the house is asleep.

Baroness starts. Emily joins her. They sing but Emily falls asleep. Fade to black.

Scene Six

Baroness is Bored

This scene works as a series of impressionistic vignettes of an afternoon.

Emily is cleaning, as in Scene 3 and Scene 11, but more adroitly. The Baroness is distractedly reading the newspaper. Fade up. Pause.

BARONESS

　I see in the newspaper that the Duchess de Sagan is returning to Paris.

Sarcastic.

　How remarkable, the Duchess returns to Paris.

EMILY

Beat.

　Answer the door?

BARONESS

　No, thank you, Emily.

Emily goes back to her task.

BARONESS (CONT'D)

>There is a picture of her in the newspaper.

Emily comes over to look in the newspaper.

>See? A photograph.

Emily reacts to an expected flash.

BARONESS (CONT'D)

>No, Emily. Here in the newspaper. You see?

Emily very warily approaches the paper, as if it were going to flash. Looks and doesn't see anything.

BARONESS (CONT'D)

>You see? It's the Duchess.

The Baroness holds up the newspaper, pointing to the photograph. Emily looks, but doesn't get it.

EMILY

>Duchess de Sagan.

BARONESS

>Yes.

Emily delicately tears the paper open on the photo as if looking for something inside.

Lights snap down, then fade up.

Emily is still cleaning. The Baroness is reading the newspaper, which now has a hole in it.

BARONESS (CONT'D)

Sighing and putting the paper down.

> Well. The newspaper, the Duchess. I don't care anymore. I don't even want to go out.

EMILY

Stops cleaning.

> Go out.

BARONESS

> Perhaps, later this afternoon.

Glances down at newspaper.

BARONESS (CONT'D)

> No doubt the Baron would have been attending the exhibition of moving pictures.

Emily gets back to cleaning the knives. The Baroness is sitting looking bored. Pause. She distractedly pokes, plays with, folds the newspaper.

Lights fade down, then snap up.

Baroness has made a small (finger sized) paper hat. She has it on her finger. Pause.

BARONESS (CONT'D)

> Look, Emily.

Emily turns, comes over.

BARONESS (CONT'D)

> You see.

Showing off the paper hat.

> The Baron used to wear a very silly-looking hat like this when he was an admiral, in the navy. You see. It's the Baron.

Emily looks, goes back to work.

Lights fade down, then snap up.

Baroness sits on the sofa wearing a (full-size) paper hat. Pause. she gets up and checks herself in the mirror.

BARONESS

> Emily?

Baroness attempts an impersonation of the Baron but she keeps breaking up. She sees Emily doesn't quite recognize her, and is slightly fearful.

> It's a hat.

She takes the hat off and puts it on Emily.

BARONESS (CONT'D)

> See! Look in the mirror.

Takes Emily to the mirror. They stand together looking in mirror.

EMILY

   Tray.

BARONESS

   Mirror.

EMILY

   Tray.

BARONESS

   Alright it's a tray. You see? There we both are in the tray.

Lights fade down.

Scene Seven

Emily Dances

Fade-up lights on Emily standing looking in the mirror. She begins to dance and sing on her own with her blanket. Continue, then she suddenly smells something and gets scared. Fade to black.

Scene Eight

Second Rape

The Baroness agonizing in a corridor outside Emily's room. She (and we) hear Emily screaming in pain—the rape is taking place and the Baroness feels (is) powerless to prevent it. She is utterly anguished.

The Baron leaves/has left.

The Baroness makes up her mind and enters Emily's room. Lights up on Emily there sitting on her bed, wrapped in her blanket, rocking in pain. The Baroness sits at the end of the bed, lost in her own unpleasant thoughts.

BARONESS

    Perhaps you should lie down.

Emily doesn't respond.

BARONESS (CONT'D)

    You could rest.

Emily slowly stops rocking. Pause. Baroness is at a loss, then carefully lays her head on Emily.

Scene Nine

Second Park Scene

Emily sitting on her blanket, unpacking the picnic basket, first her boots, then the tray, then Shakespeare's Julius Caesar. *Finally an apple.*

The Baroness is sitting, staring out, lost. A woman without hope and on the edge of despair.

EMILY

Holding out the apple.

    Dinner?

BARONESS

   No thank you.

Emily starts to eat it then pauses. She looks at the Baroness. The Baroness realizes Emily is watching her thoughtfully.

Takes attention away from herself by pointing to ducks.

   Quack.

EMILY

Duck noise.

   Quack.

She's correcting the Baroness.

   Qua-ack.

BARONESS

Tries to get it right.

   Qua-ack.

EMILY

   Quack.

BARONESS

   Quack.

Emily is satisfied. She eats on, sniffs. She notices something a distance away.

EMILY

Strong cow imitation.

Moo...

BARONESS

Turns and looks.

Oh yes. Cows.

EMILY

Moo...

BARONESS

They're cows, Emily. Cows?

EMILY

Cows.

Beat.

Moo...

BARONESS

Obliged, deep breath.

Moo.

And she does it quite well.

Emily is satisfied. Pause.

Emily is getting bored. She starts to sing obviously trying to get the Baroness interested. The Baroness turns and smiles but goes back to her dark thoughts. Emily, discouraged, stops.

EMILY

Sing?

Baroness shakes her head. Back to thoughts. Emily looking out makes a train noise.

EMILY (CONT'D)

   Train.

BARONESS

   Yes, Emily. It's a train.

Nothing else happens. Emily gets bored again.

EMILY

   Act?

BARONESS

   What?

EMILY

Holds up book.

   Julius Caesar?

Baroness shakes her head.

Emily takes the book and quietly "reads" from it, nonsense talk, doing her version of the Baroness's Shakespearean acting. Her strategy when at first not noticed is to gradually get larger and louder. Baroness is too preoccupied to get involved with Emily. Emily gives up.

EMILY (CONT'D)

   Hat. Hat?

Holds out her finger.

BARONESS

Beat.

    Alright.

Baroness makes a little hat, Emily puts it on the finger of one hand.

EMILY

    Baron.

She holds up her other hand, wiggles the fingers.

    Conspirators.

She begins a kind of puppet show. "Baron" is very nasty, scaring the conspirators and then Emily.

By this time the Baroness is moderately engaged in this amusing pageant.

The "conspirators" begin to conspire . . .

EMILY (CONT'D)

Speaking for Baron.

    Oh, grovel, grovel, grovel . . .

Improv.

    ". . . Blood of ordinary man . . ."

Improv. Speaking for the conspirators.

    "I kiss thy hand, but not in flattery, great Caesar."

The conspirators "kiss" Baron/Caesar's hand.

EMILY (CONT'D)

Speaking for a very pompous Julius Caesar.

"I move and pray..."

Improv.

"...Northern Star..."

Improv.

"...Shining fire."

The Baroness is entertained. The conspirator fingers stalk the Baron finger. It gets tense—involved. Suddenly a large sharp knife is out of the picnic basket and the conspirator fingers are holding it.

To the fixed horror of the Baroness, Emily very deliberately cuts a slit down her Baron finger. Beat.

EMILY (CONT'D)

Quietly.

Murder.

She puts her ear to her the bleeding finger which slowly wilts.

EMILY (CONT'D)

Dead.

She holds out her finger for the Baroness to listen. The Baroness is frozen, not just from the sight of the wound but from understanding that what was a game is also a murder plot (the only way Emily could communicate it). Emily takes back her finger, licks it, then holds it out again to the Baroness.

EMILY (CONT'D)

Very deliberately, a contract.

    Lick?

Long pause as the Baroness stares at finger. Then she slowly leans forward and licks it.

Scene Ten

Emily Murders the Baron

Suggestion: The Baroness waits and waits in semi-dark. Finally Emily appears and hands a large bloody knife to her and she wraps it in a large piece of cloth that she's been holding. But please go much more elaborate if you wish. Use a little imagination.

Scene Eleven

Final Song

Baroness addresses the audience standing beside the sofa where Emily sits, dead centre. There is something reminiscent of her preparations in Scene 1 and 7. They both could be wearing black arm bands.

BARONESS

> As we gather here this evening there is of course a cloud that hangs over us all, when we recall the tragic and untimely death of my late husband, the Baron. This evening however I would simply like you to recall his courage, his gallantry, when, hearing an intruder in the servants quarters he went at dead of night to the aid of our sleeping

maid Emily. Thus I found him, in the room there, stabbed through the heart . . .

EMILY

Quietly to herself.

Julius Caesar . . .

BARONESS

. . . by the assassin who then fled, unapprehended.

Beat.

But, after a suitable period of mourning, I think we best show our respect for the dead by taking up again those things which give depth and meaning to our brief lives. It is in this spirit that I present Emily to sing for us.

Emily as many of you now know, was rescued from the milieu of wild beasts to become my maid. I have become very fond of her. And tonight we will show how such a one can come to beauty as well as service.

Emily stands and gives a short rendering of the song Connais-tu le pays *from the opera* Mignon *by Ambroise Thomas.*

The Baroness applauds enthusiastically. They pose for the final portrait, Baroness and maid. Emily closes her eyes.

FLASH. *Blackout.*

END

Staging

There are major challenges in staging *The Baroness and the Pig*; in the transitions, the communication of certain non-verbal aspects of the story (see for example, the mirror-recognition scene at the end of Act One and the murder scene towards the end of Act Two). I've seen—in Hungarian, German and French productions—imaginative and very different solutions to these. So if you decide to stage this play, come up with a few yourself. The play is written in two acts but can be performed without intermission. Its usual running time (without a break) seems to be about 1 hour 20 minutes.

For notes on photography and *enfant sauvage* (two themes of the play) see the production notes at the beginning of this edition. —M.M.

Also from Rock's Mills Press

ANNE'S HOUSE OF DREAMS
Annotated Edition

L.M. Montgomery
Edited and with an introduction and notes by Jen Rubio

Anne of Green Gables, newly married to doctor Gilbert Blythe, settles in the village by the sea of Glen St. Mary, Prince Edward Island, where she befriends the enigmatic and unforgettably beautiful Leslie Moore. Glen St. Mary is a fascinating community with eccentric, unpredictable characters, from the sharp-tongued Cornelia Bryant to the great humanist and storyteller, Captain Jim Boyd. Montgomery's depiction of life in this village includes haunting descriptions of the land and seascape, in which a series of human tragedies and comedies unfold. *Anne's House of Dreams* is perhaps the most personal of Montgomery's novels, reflecting events and experiences she recorded in her private journals. This Rock's Mills Press edition includes the following features:

- Introduction by Jen Rubio exploring the novel in the context of the newly published edition of *L.M. Montgomery's Complete Journals: The Ontario Years, 1911-1917*
- New notes, unique to this edition, explaining such terms as "the shadow of Venus," "old Scratch," and Abegweit, as well as historical references such as the failed Bank of Prince Edward Island and the Wartime Elections Act
- Reproductions of original photographs that scholars believe are some of the locations featured in the novel.

Paperback, 208 pages
ISBN-13: 978-1-77244-040-9

www.rocksmillspress.com

Also from Rock's Mills Press

RILLA OF INGLESIDE
Annotated Edition

L.M. Montgomery
Edited and with an introduction and notes by Jen Rubio

"There is absolutely no one around here who seems to realize the war. I believe it is well they do not. If all felt as I do over it the work of the country would certainly suffer." In her journal entry for January 1, 1915, L.M. Montgomery lamented the absence of close companions with whom to discuss the war in her new life as a minister's wife in the rural community of Leaskdale, Ontario. Montgomery would work hard throughout the war years, contributing to the war effort as well as helping her husband in his role as minister. But there were few people with whom she could discuss the terrible events of the time. Instead, she carefully and quietly recorded war news in her journals. Two years after the war ended, she used this material to write *Rilla of Ingleside* – a novel about endurance and sacrifice on the Canadian home front. Here, characters follow the international conflict closely and share the experience of fear, dread, and loss. Rilla matures during the war years, learning to endure hard work and loneliness, and the death of her beloved brother Walter (Walter is widely accepted to be a fictional version of John McCrae, the Canadian soldier who composed "In Flanders Fields").

New notes based on the latest research about Canada in World War I show that Montgomery's analysis of war was surprisingly accurate. This new edition adds to our knowledge of Montgomery as well as Canada's role in the war, and features two rare photos, one which appears to have been the inspiration for Rilla, the other for Rilla's fiance.

Paperback, 380 pages
ISBN-13: 978-1-77244-011-9

www.rocksmillspress.com

Also from Rock's Mills Press

EMILY OF NEW MOON
Annotated Edition

L.M. Montgomery
Edited and with an introduction and notes by Jen Rubio

It had always seemed to Emily, ever since she could remember, that she was very, very near to a world of wonderful beauty. Between it and herself hung only a thin curtain; she could never draw the curtain aside—but sometimes, just for a moment, a wind fluttered it and then it was as if she caught a glimpse of the enchanting realm beyond—only a glimpse—and heard a note of unearthly music.

When Emily's father dies and she is left orphaned, she must go live with relatives at the New Moon Farm on Prince Edward Island. Emily is a deeply sensitive child; few of her proud Presbyterian relatives approve of her "artistic temperament."

New Moon is a fascinating old farmstead that Emily grows to love, full of tradition and story and beauty. But unlike Green Gables, there are dark shadows: tales of insanity, anger, bitterness, and betrayal are woven in the narrative quilt that Emily inherits. Drawn in particular to one of the dark stories that has left an undercurrent of anger and sadness into the lives of those around her, Emily finds ways of exploring the depth of human experience on her journey to artistic knowledge.

Written in 1923, during Montgomery's years in Leaskdale, Ontario, this novel about childhood glimpses into the often dark and mysterious world of adult life explores artistic perception in a way unlike any of Montgomery's other novels. Echoes of Emily can be found in other major works of female bildungsromaner, like Alice Munro's *The Lives of Girls and Women* and Margaret Laurence's *The Diviners*.

This extensively annotated edition includes dozens of notes that illuminate the historical and literary background to the novel, illuminating its complexity and meaning in a completely new and revealing way. Vintage photographs relating to the novel's setting are also included.

Paperback, 266 pages
ISBN-13: 978-1-77244-056-0

Also from Rock's Mills Press

IN THE MIDST OF ALARMS

Robert Barr
Introduction and Notes by Jen Rubio

An exciting new annotated edition of the only novel ever published that depicts the 1866 invasion of British-ruled Canada by Irish republicans, an event that would help set the stage for Confederation ...

New notes provide fascinating insight into this intriguing narrative of Canadian-American relations. The two countries clash in this fast-paced comedy of manners by Scottish-Canadian-American writer Robert Barr (1849–1912). In 1866, a group of Irish-Americans known as the Fenian Brotherhood carried out cross-border raids into British-ruled Canada. The main reason was to take over Canada—or part of it—in order to hold it hostage, with a view to forcing Britain's political exit from Ireland. Battle-hardened veterans fresh from fighting in the American Civil War crossed the border, and were surprised by the resistance they met. In the context of the novel, a vacationing American journalist is equally surprised by feisty Canadians who are ever willing to push back against stereotypes.

It is no coincidence that Confederation took place the year following the raids, as Canadians realized their vulnerability to invasion.

Author Robert Barr (1849–1912) moved from Scotland to Toronto with his parents at age four. After two decades as a teacher in Windsor, he moved to the U.S. where he became news editor of the *Detroit Free Press*.

Paperback, 280 pages
ISBN-13: 978-1-77244-001-0

www.rocksmillspress.com

Also from Rock's Mills Press
Three Novels by Hamilton Author Peter Abbot

HAMILTONIANS

Two brutal slayings—dubbed the "Millennial Murders" by the media—have shocked residents of Steeltown. But that's only the beginning …

In this new novel, Peter Abbot, himself a long-time resident of Canada's tenth largest city, explores the meaning of hope, despair, and redemption—and introduces readers to a number of Hamiltonians they won't soon forget.

Paperback, 220 pages
ISBN-13: 978-1-77244-126-0 / 978-1-77244-127-7 (Amazon)

VOICE OF THE LORD

Zimbabwe, 1983.

Three young people—one from Australia, one from Canada, and one from Britain—visit the country once known as Rhodesia in the wake of its achievement of black majority rule.

But the ghosts of the country's troubled past have not yet been laid to rest, as Paul, Susanna and Stephen will soon discover.

Voice of the Lord is a compelling exploration of the heart of darkness within us all, as well as of the enduring power of poetry to explain and heal.

Paperback, 186 pages
ISBN-13: 978-1-77244-031-7

LIBRARIAN

Last man on earth—I'm beginning to fantasize that. The last human survivor! Seems very unlikely, in a world inhabited by so many millions of people in so many cities, so many countries. But in this silence—who knows? Actually, I think it's the silence, and my deepening sense of isolation, that are encouraging me to think I may be alone, completely alone.

So begins *Librarian*, a compelling short novel of survival and the search for meaning, filled with fascinating characters and thought-provoking meditations on the meaning of philosophy and literature in a world gone wrong.

Paperback, 102 pages
ISBN-13: 978-1-77244-017-1

www.rocksmillspress.com

Also from Rock's Mills Press
Two Novels by Cayuga Author John Passfield

BETHUNE: THE ONLY PERSON ALIVE IN THE WORLD

Southwestern Ontario author John Passfield has embarked on a project to explore the concepts of form and meaning in the novel, as well as the place of the novel as a form of expression in the 21st century. *Bethune: The Only Person Alive in the World* is among the most recent entries in the project. In the novel, readers follow Canadian doctor Norman Bethune as his social conscience takes him on a journey through the Canada of the Great Depression, the Spain of the Spanish Civil War, and the China of the Chinese Civil War and Japanese invasion.

Paperback, 158 pages
ISBN-13: 978-1-77244-093-5

JOB: THE CORNERSTONE OF THE UNIVERSE

Devastated by the loss of his family, Job cries out to the heavens. Why has God forsaken him? Why is the universe so flawed? His agony has given him the questions. He insists on hearing the answers from the mouth of God.

Paperback, 144 pages
ISBN-13: 978-1-77244-079-9

www.rocksmillspress.com

Also from Rock's Mills Press

WATERSHED
Judith Love

Ranging in time from the late 1960s to the present day, *Watershed* is the story of Anne Macleod, a young Ottawa public servant who finds her life caught up in the tumultuous events of her time—Trudeaumania, the FLQ crisis, and Quebec separatism. Finding love only to lose it, she is later confronted with a decades-old mystery, with her efforts to unravel it leading to new and surprising revelations. *Watershed* is a novel both of intriguing characterization and one that is evocative of times and places that still resonate in the Canadian experience.

Judith Love worked for many years for the Public Service of Canada in Ottawa and Nova Scotia, primarily helping to implement Canada's official languages policy and employment initiatives for women, Indigenous peoples and people with disabilities. While living in Botswana in the late 1980s, she served as an advisor to the Secretary General of the Red Cross. More recently, Love has tutored international students and new immigrants in Nova Scotia and Ottawa. She currently lives in Wolfville, Nova Scotia.

Paperback, 260 pages
ISBN-13: 978-1-77244-111-6 / 978-1-77244-110-9 (Amazon)

Also from Rock's Mills Press

IT CAN'T HAPPEN HERE

Sinclair Lewis
With a New Preface by Robert Bothwell

"Lewis's [character] Windrip is a version of a rising demagogue of that time [Huey Long].... Three-quarters of a century ago, Lewis argued that fascism and totalitarianism could happen here. Could it?"
Chicago Tribune, March 2016

"Election year 2016 like election year 1936 offered an opportunity for Tea Party doctrines to find expression, a leader and a majority.... Trump appealed to ... people who longed for a simpler past in which there were no disturbing minorities, the sky was blue, and the convertible was filled with cheap gas."
From Robert Bothwell's Preface

Sinclair Lewis's 1935 novel remains jaw-droppingly readable with its account of populism, politics, and power in America. This new edition features a lively preface by Robert Bothwell, who draws some fascinating parallels between the political atmosphere of 1935 and that of 2016. The connections are striking: so-called politically incorrect "everyman" rhetoric, Revolutionary War symbolism, and even the nervous belief that "It Can't Happen Here."

Sinclair Lewis (1885–1951) was a novelist, short-story writer, and playwright. He was the first American to receive the Nobel Prize for literature. Robert Bothwell is director of the International Relations program at Trinity College at the University of Toronto, and a leading authority on relations between Canada and the United States.

Paperback, 268 pages
ISBN-13: 978-1-77244-030-0

www.rocksmillspress.com

www.ingramcontent.com/pod-product-compliance
Lightning Source LLC
Chambersburg PA
CBHW030913080526
44589CB00010B/280